Zen and the Art of Astroturf

Bronwyn Rodden

WYNDOW BOOKS

Acknowledgements:

These poems were first published in the following journals:

Tuesday, only its Monday – Muse, Friendly Street Reader
Glass Boxes – Friendly Street Reader
Floating – UTS Anthology 13th Floor
Death of a Party Animal – Island
Lambmarking – Scarp
Fire Days (extract)– NPWS Journal
There's no bells, it's just the sound of lanterns in Chinatown – Redoubt
The White Plumed Honeyeater – The Bimblebox Project
Return of the Shearwaters – 142 New Zealand and Australian Poets, Light on Don Banks
Last Days at Work – Refractory Girl

Cover photo by Bronwyn Rodden

ISBN: 9798759231202

© Bronwyn Rodden 2021. All rights reserved. No part of this publication may be reproduced, stored in or introduced into a retrieval system, or transmitted, in any form or by any means (electronic, mechanical, photocopying, recording or otherwise), without the prior written permission of the author.

www.wyndowbooks.com

Contents

Zen and the art of Astroturf	1
Tuesday, only it's Monday	3
Glass Boxes	4
The house is breathing	5
Controlled Burn in Eden	6
For Jenny	11
Meat tray raffles are back	13
Floating	14
The Chance of it Happening	16
Learning to draw through bus windows	17
Shawl	19
Death of a Party Animal	22
Lunch at Berowra	24
Exit	26
Dead chicken-meat day	27
Inside Out	28
Dubbo Perspectives	29
Words stolen from an unfinished poem by Lauren Williams	36
Addict	37
The Loaded Dog – Fitzroy (now luxury apartments)	40
Lily of the Valley Ladies	42
Christmas, lost in our own minds	44
'sadly missed'	46
Cartwheeling	49
Adaptation	50
Lamb-marking	56

Fire Days – January	58
Two Red Chickens	75
The valley of soundless trees: Wollombi	76
The White Plumed Honeyeater	78
bee yellow native	79
Winter	80
Garden	81
There are no bells, it's just the sound of restaurant lanterns in Chinatown	82
Mountain track alone	87
Myall Lakes	88
River Swim	90
Return of the Shearwaters	92
Spring at Bronte	93
Unchanging territory - The Snowy, for Mike	94
Last Days at Work	97

Zen and the art of Astroturf

In the dry sort of wind
        that leaves no chance
no trace on you like
a passing lover
        I make for the trees
           to block out the offices I go into
because everyone else is there.

The lawn at the uni
        is shaved like astro turf
and there are blotches in the usual
end   of   year   party   places.
Coming and going is serious
        these few weeks before it all starts again.
I'm just visiting.

In the library I try and try
to cram in all the poets and storytellers but
           I can't seem to touch them.
Outside again
        the sun scuttles fast from my back
swift as the wind, or the touch of passing love.

Into the quad for shelter:
      I'm joined by a swarm of starlings
    who don't belong here, either
            their wings translucent and stubby.

I toss a discarded
         five
              cent
                    piece.   Tails.

Dylan Thomas wanted to write poetry big enough for people to walk around,
    or make love to:
        substitution or extrapolation?
I may be on the mountain
unable to see   where I am.

Tuesday, only it's Monday

They've only just realised the cat outside the takeaway food bar is dead.
The old man saw it, stood, like I did, looking at its body curled-up like normal.
Then the nearby smudge, not much, hardly any blood at all and the eyes, half-open.
He called his fat son to look and they stood with hands in pockets then walked back inside.

The bus is the one after the one that's supposed to have arrived.
My complaint confirms to the driver that I have just come from Neptune.
I wouldn't mind so much if the sky wasn't the colour of Dad's eyes that day
just like the cat's, half-open and dead.

Glass Boxes

In the dusty armchair afternoon
I remember slate skies and fingers
Turning white or was it just a shadow
As I sit protected, away from them all.

They live in glass boxes which
Sometimes I open or sometimes
They spring from them with night eyes.
And there are others, high up

In the forgotten house with sun
Tearing at its sides and I have
To climb the stairs and try the doors.
There are some who will always be there.

Outside, there is a garden through
Finger-grimed glass and the sky is not
Grey but blue. But there's no sound so
The trees are pictures and the birds, poems.

the house is breathing

the house is breathing
the walls move in and out
a dog pretends he's just outside
neighbours sense something
step evenly across our path
the day is hollow   way out
its edges are consolidating
and nobody hears the hum
in the air

Controlled Burn in Eden

I am in Eden, early,
sunlight melts icy blades,
a long low tide reveals
a bed for waterbirds;
gulls, godwits and oystercatchers
scooping their jet heads
for crustaceans,
parrots stir a rumpus in the trees
others collide more quietly,
trills, whistles broken
by the whipbirds' crack;
singular and defiant.

Last night in Eden
I borrowed overalls and boots
joined our local people
on the line
in controlled burning,
for politics and the forest,
the darkness
closing us together
our faces reflecting
the flames,

the unknown factor of Eden
with us in the night.

Nature isn't tamed here;
the Sacred Ibis
don't eat our garbage,
birds of all sizes
fly sensibly from us,
bellbirds have begun
to chime near the town.

We walked around Eden
in twos laying trails
of liquid fire,
brushing through low scrub
past windrows piled up
wrongly under tall trees,
it means they'll burn badly,
the boss explained:
the first fire takes the bark
the second burns deeper,
the softer flesh,
then more and more until
it's just a hollow
waiting for flame.

With me in Eden

you spoke of the bush,

rolling wisdom off your tongue,

reams of experience,

we shared our lives -

mine in the city.

You ask:

What would you be

doing tonight

if you were at home?

Not this.

Our words are measured

by my clumping boots,

and reality,

but the taste of electricity

is in the air.

In Eden the beauty

can carry you away,

there are smells you

never smell in the office,

colours which aren't real

in the city.

But we're old enough

to understand deception,

like triggers from

tracks that seem familiar
but lead you astray,
distorting your coordinates,
lousing up your grid references.

I joined the other women
on the fire truck,
we could be anywhere:
on a shopping cue,
or a hospital ward,
in a rice field
weighed down
with huge baskets,
a baby somewhere near us
if not on a back;
it's all surprisingly the same.

Here in Eden
they're serious in their work,
passionate for the care
of our inheritance,
we trace again and again
the progress of our fire,
finally giving up

on gullies too damp
to light up.
The truck swerves,
a tiny antechinus runs
frightened from our wheels.

This morning in Eden
I'm blinded by the colours
of rosellas and lorikeets
tussling in wild, red gum flowers
like the fire's heart,
far from the night air,
the fertile lushness
of the forest.
My Eden,
that collection of sensations
like the sun now
eating through my clothes
thawing the morning-walk cold,
brings blood to my face,
like fire.

For Jenny

A face develops in the clouds and she resists
its growing familiarity; it's a man, a boy, both.
They look at her from the same eyes. If only
they would take their storm-blue faces away.
She watches the changing features wrestle the sky.

Then, the slap of wood, hollow wood;
no longer sluiced by channels of existence,
breath and moisture are gone from the shell
now aged, emaciated, a withered board
bent in a salty wind. Part of a house,

Its nailed frame hidden from rains
which slice their course from hilltop to sea.
Shafts of sun pierce the glassy streams,
their cargoes of green and lustrous yellow
a vibration of petals and leaves and water.

Closing her eyes, she is surrounded by the wind
howling at nothing, more tangible in darkness
than in light, it whirls with long-ago seashells
in bright, sandy days of childhood, plastic buckets
and castles with sandy turrets in the wind.

Wind that blew sails on boats made of paper
and sticks ploughing their courses on the
streams that run everywhere in childhood
and in stories of places which ceased to exist
now that she was grown. No more, no more.

She opened her eyes and the wind died.
The faces were once more clouds and fell away.
The sun was hot and real on the grass,
the sound only the shutters. Through
the window a chair, a room, a home.

Meat tray raffles are back

Down at the beach
pushed aside the syringes
careful with the needles
all of us in the bus
look up at the first
skeleton of the new bridge
people at the DMR viewing platform
bend necks
it looks taller than Centrepoint
I think of John's Blackwattle Bay
being obscured
gradually and rationally
it sends signals up the itchy feet nerves
we'll move on
hop-skipping the tricky bits of the city

the sun is really
making itself felt today
and
meat tray raffles are back
every Thursday and Friday
men walk babies
and there's no-one lying in the street today.

Floating*

above is the allusion
but they don't.
They're fixed in amusing poses
or fucked.
Geishas, Courtesans
the gallery signs say coyly
not prostitutes.

A sea of porcelain dolls
no sign of life
but their exposed genitals
recorded with forensic accuracy
better than dental records
of course, their clients'
pricks are huge
beyond belief.

Oh, oh,
a face has slipped by with
an expression:
`After Bathing`
the artist couldn't ignore
her tedium.

One retired woman

proclaimed each of her years at least

as difficult as the Zen master's.

Damura stared at the wall

for nine

she stared at the ceiling

for ten:

Geishaness next to Godliness?

the difference being

as always, choice.

From "The Floating World" Japanese prints ("women") exhibition (19C-about), AGNSW July, 1994.

The Chance of it Happening

Chi-squared is a mathematics man
He does his x's like two c's joined
And writes little numbers
Above and below all sorts of words
To emphasise or de-emphasise.

You will see him on a hill,
Amidst the scents of virile spring,
Squinting through glasses at a page
Of black and white numbers,
A bird may land,
A butterfly wither,
He does not see.

He could tell you
The likelihood of it happening
But never how he can enjoy
Because enjoyment is in the
Squinting and if you don't
Like it you don't know what it is
To squint, and he too busy to explain.

Learning to draw through bus windows

I

pink and fluffy if only she would wear red

she wouldn't cough so much I'm sure

what chance has pink angora

against reflections and pebblecrete

strained natives creep around pots

lifting an occasional flowerhead

teethrot drinkcans drain dregs onto fine tendrils

colour too much too much too too

all over sliding around corners at me

get away get away

don't sell me the news in Iraq America

I want to know about the toothache next door

sleazy glass shiny eyes synthesised from the morning sun (30th to 35th floor)

II

tides of people stream scream at me

it's 8.45 am

the Wynyard penseller is a headless tracksuit on wheels,

laboratory flowers threaten

the mail man (person) growls over his trolley

bicycle boys' legs are at the stockexchangeready

merciless cars threaten us at the crossing

in Wagga we gave money for Bangladesh

at work the talk is about the air

it was in the paper

Shawl

She is walking,
wrapped like an apostle
among the candles
burning and puffing to extinction
in a blanket made
by a woman.

I could never have been an apostle
she says
there's nothing for me in churches.

She winds it around her flesh
it warms her
unlike marble.
Being weak is strength
she says
but that's no excuse
for being weak.

Apostlebirds move in groups of 12 or so
for safety.

I'm the old woman

trudging in my shawl

there's power in its

sway around my body

the fullness of it enveloping me

making me large.

I tie myself up in it

and decide when I will

untie it.

Stones are cold.

Arranged in a certain way

the space around them

can grow warm

but not the stones.

A face carved in them is dead.

I'm on the wet coast

break, break, break,

hair stretched and pulled by the wind

I draw my clothes tight around me

look down to the shore below

at the rocks.

The weather drives against me
but it's full of electricity and
I bundle it up in my shawl
just enough for a week or two
and head home.
I light a candle for silence
let the fire dry me
and loosen my shawl.

Death of a Party Animal for Chris, in memoriam

amber leaves shine among green
each day another dies
your ambering has left you empty

no pictures in your mind
saves you from the pain
of absent family

then a brother you've not seen
in twenty years made a call
morphine distracted you from the tears

autumn is the time for you to die
you won't believe it
so you are saved from

considering your last summer
if it's particularly full of light
by the permanent blue sea

you say
I must go to the mountains
once more   do cocktails

but it's your funeral
they should always be on rainy days
it seems only fair

the sea swirls behind a glass wall
to distract me I think of you
out there with the gulls

the wood of the coffin is pale
the bearers surprised it's so light
but the weight of you is not there

friends walk away
in a small group
treading carefully

Lunch at Berowra

At the tea-house
the sun scrounged around puggy trees
an ungreen reflection in the
hard restless water
that could swallow a body without a sigh.

Purple light touched lines
in the corners of our faces -
from age, flesh memories -
we talk of perfect trees
historical interesting incidents.

We come for the isolation
the far-fromness of a frail weatherboard womb
in the body of a natural reserve
there's a mirror for voyeurs
and rustic Australiana strewn comfortingly.
Around and around the meal
are smiling winebaked faces.
In need of a walk we move on,
rain forest frosts the fingers
like the scent of sex in the woods.

Urgently we enjoy, before the sun
drops behind mountain boulders
a man halloes his wife and it returns to him
a parrot shouts our outsiderness,
cusping the expanse of the Hawkesbury.

We bank on our belief of Australianness
and how it belongs to us and we to it
at last not drifting populations on a floating island
but the glare is intimidating and we
can't see for the sun, can't feel for the wind.

Exit

The sky is choked with thick clouds,
what are you doing now?
I allow myself to think of your pale eyes in the moody pub,
the curve of muscle on your neck.

I look at the sunshine on wooden beams of a house way out, away:
could we have had something like that -
sun quiet in the west over millions of undisturbed trees,
your eyes so soft.

Did I want it? Peace after a walk in the delicate bush,
swooshed with tree ferns, observed by an ambling wedgetail,
your arms, that vein running from
your forefinger to your elbow.

Sun touches a hill, hollowing, carving it
into a tactile vision; this sunset,
you'll watch it
from the airport lounge.

dead chicken-meat day

the sign says
two skinned chickens for 6 dollars

a man furtively delivers
a heavy carton
to the charcoal chicken
shop.

I have to pass KFC panting
essence of cooked chook
to get to work

at the car yard a yellow beak pokes from a racing suit

in the office I overhear:
excuse me Carol,
I've got Channel 7 on the phone
they want to do something about

the release

                of domestic

                                ducks

Inside Out

Tracey liked her name when
it was said by mother, father,
sister, brother. She didn't
mind when it was said by
school friends and boyfriends.
When it started being said by
teacher and prefect and mother
in the same tones she started
not to like it. When it was
said by policewomen and lawyers
and doctors and magistrates
like her mother she started
to hate it. When it was said
by gaolers and nurses and
psychologists and the gaol mother
and the gaol bullies she
began to disbelieve it. When
it was said late at night
in an ugly voice that froze
the lonely second she disowned it.
One day she saw it dark and fresh
tattooed above a woman's breast
and it was real after all.

Dubbo Perspectives

Strips of burning red,
the western soil cuts through
flooded paddocks,
we fly over, curve into it,
a flock of grey wool is rolling
along a straight red line
like soap suds;
uneven and wavering.

We talk, allies, of differences,
black and white,
husband and wife,
police and corruption,
the bite of anger still
in you from years ago
I marvel as you explain
the landholder's power
to call the cops
any name under the sun;
didn't leave home for years,
did you, says Sally.

Politics is a possibility
it all fits
you've reached that point
where you're tired of
the rush of control
outgrown your area
have learnt to manipulate,
had the drunken officials
in the palm of your hand.
"We beat them"
and so you did.
You have many ideas
good and worthy
respecting neither law nor clergy.

You fashion your world
in your image as you
feed out your cattle
on the weekend,
understand better than most
the concept of Aboriginals
reclaiming control,
and how people give it away
for a smile, a grin,
a reasoned argument

in a strong voice.
A woman doesn't always win
using these tricks,
nor can she drink the
opposition under the table.

Sheep roll like water
here and there at the
bark of the dogs,
nip of the heel.
We're on the edge, here,
a sliver of city-shined humanity
next to the desert,
we all know it's out there
huge, dangerous,
explorers aren't remembered
for nothing.

More climbers have been
claimed by Everest today,
"don't worry too much…"
one said, calling by cellular phone
from the end of his life.
Knowing it's out there
makes it feel like

a vast chasm we could

all slip into, unless

we keep control.

Farmers, landholders,

know how the land

isn't there forever

unaided, unchanging,

it needs watching, keeping,

like an animal, or it

will slip away from you

fall back to less than nature -

it can never really go back.

The sheep flow down the red paths,

like soft flocculations down drainpipes

moving at the sound of a bark,

the nip of a heel.

I'm in the country,

my towel from last night

is bone dry,

the bathroom window fills with

an already strong blue sky

and yellow sun;

Autumn

you can tell from the steam.

I worry about all this water
remember Tibooburra
in the shearer's quarters
instructions about the rainwater shower
and the big treat that the newlyweds
brought back from the 'Hill -
ice-cream.
I made them banana splits.

But this is Dubbo, a motel,
tourists want water.
There was some flooding,
so I relax.
The police came around
accusing you of sheep stealing,
an insurance claim,
you take them to the top of a hill,
hundreds of grey bundles
spread out across the valley,
`go find them' you say,
your brother refusing
to send a dog around.

It's nearly June,
still, we're inland,
I know outside there's a day
that'll fill my insides with hope
burning sun and a chill that
brings your face alive.
I sit in bed relishing no need
to rise early
(no commuting necessary)
but then there's the birds
I can't ignore a raucous parrot,
teasing me to get out there
with it,
a man in the next room
blows his nose loudly and
a cockie outside replies.

I go down to the river
past the gardens of Dubbo
Autumning,
It's too close to traffic
but there's a whooping pigeon,
the water's flat and mirrors
the inevitable willows
but there are majestic gums too

when you're on the ground
and can see them.

The deception ends as you hit ground,
everything's larger,
the roads stretch wide from side to side
it would take four of us to hold hands
around this ghost-trunk
and there's the air...
Herons, honeyeaters, a treecreeper
at least two birds I don't know
and the chuckling of lorikeets.
People passing in cars see
a woman by a road
looking up into the trees.

Words stolen from an unfinished poem by Lauren Williams

I'm borrowing your old racehorse
the one who bolts at the sight of an open stretch
a runway, a freeway,
"remembering as it goes along to get faster"
for it's a perfect companion to my elephant

at the zoo, my head full of Tarzan and native drums
mesmerized by its majestic dimensions
the slow, rotating monolith of a head, I almost left
when it began

one giant tortoise-leg lifted up and somewhere,
from a youth of circuses, came a dance,
one foot then another, swaying its
gentle old back from side to side,
then, as if a tap had been turned off somewhere,
it stopped, one foot in the air.

As I run down my latest racetrack
dancing my same old dances
I begin to wonder.

Addict

Sunday slabs the week again
wind death-white and hasty
cut the thread of responsibility
lay me with a voice of fiction
gimme a line

Stranded like a paw in milk
push it all outside again
joy-ride straight to heaven
who cares what the point is
gimme a line

Round the circle dragging
fifteen housemaids on their knees
push them through the windswill holes
paint them in your Rembrandt-ese
gimme a line

Hurtle down town into it
fleshy knives make stories stick
coloured scarlet, purple, white,
Tiger Tiger burning bright
gimme a line

Salutations on frosty moons
Catherine's calling for the bored
Dorothy scolds the sheep on track
Williams in the flowers again
gimme a line

Star knight star bright
hit me with it curled up tight
cut and hack no-ones listening
do it slowly in your kitchen
gimme a line

Find a mountain top
mountain crater,
mountain lake
mountain monk
mountaineer
mountain devil
mountain eyrie way up high
gimme a line

Break Break Break all the
feet of your cane toads

oh see

touch the magic button

puff the magic pastry

gimme a line

Splatten satin sardine shoes

tip and touch and soon the bloom

overcame his gorgon fume

plays the Billy tailor-blue

gimme a line

gimme a line   all fall down

The Loaded Dog – Fitzroy (now luxury apartments)

Another, another rustic pub
pictures of men like Dad,
swagmen, only earlier:
a Depression swaggy.
'I carried my bluey'
he would say, after a few.
And their dogs like our's,
foxies, clever, loyal
on the road, unloaded.

Dust strewn implements are
fixed to the walls: grandpa's
bits and wooden pieces now
decorative against peach and beige.
Two old men sit near us,
with their pipes and stares,
somehow comforting.
Devil's Choice is my beer
stung with raspberries,
Lawson would have frowned
but drunk it anyway.

The fire rustles nearby
we purr in the heat:
bang! it responds.

And there are pictures
of romantic gold miners
in classic beards,
cowboy charisma,
but if you were really there -
the flies, the maggoty meat,
the unrelenting sun:
nature was something
to be protected from
Life in the bush.

Lily of the Valley Ladies

The Lily of the Valley Ladies

are disappearing

taking their

Old Country Roses

their lace hankies in boxes

from Switzerland

their lavender soap

and going.

They're heading off

into the distance

walking faster

than I give them credit for

with a gleam in their eye

that's been growing

since childhood

and contains

their Mother's smile

on her wedding day

and their Father's

at Christmas

and their own

when they first looked

into the eyes

of their child.

Christmas, lost in our own minds

Buskers are cellists now
in the Devonshire Street tunnel,
Few return to its seething
ungrateful hordes - being
trapped makes us edgy.

The train slides fast from
Redfern to Hurstville non-stop.
Working in the suburbs, a touch
of the village: lunchtime strolls
past well-tended roses, natives.

I want to see inside these
homey lives, try to make out
shapes through laced windows.
Feel like inviting myself in,
`Please, show me your lives'.

Enter the facadism of family,
careless words across paling fences,
my mother isolated in her garden,
submersed in painting and print
instead of neighbours.

Life anywhere can be stultifying,
as much as in a village.
We've come seeking freedom and spend
our time locking doors, making walls,
brick by fashionable brick.

Friday in the tunnel, the singers
do better, `Have a good weekend'
is squeezed out between footsteps
and "It's a Hard World", the jangle
of money signals celebration.

The Sallies too, it's the season.
The escalator is strangely empty
and I imagine a fear of heights
as I watch its metal scales slip,
lizardlike, into the chasm beneath.

'sadly missed'

The mark of another person
gone down the innocent cliff path
lined with tough plants
sprouting their first yellow blooms:
a car pulls up to look
a man stops in his stroll
a hang-glider flies over.

Beside the chainwire fence
a post which gave
meaning to surveyors
now points to an exit
from a troubled world;
four crosses, four lives,
silk flowers –
promising eternity,
pale against the Pacific.

Lumbering tankers
their rusty ballast lines
bright, almost cheerful,
slide by, far away,
a body falling
would not be seen
from their decks.

The safe path for joggers
meanders past a bench
where I sit wondering
why the sea always
reminds me of death,
this habit of wreath-placing
welding it further in.

Friday and the sky is clear
just a ripple of low cloud
and half a thin moon
enough breeze
to clear out the head
and ripple silk petals
'30 years, sadly missed'
I hope they were good ones.

Most deaths from cliffs
would be at night
blind to your destiny below
there's just the release
as you step out
into the wind that will
never bother you again.

A pelican whoomps over
unaware of vertigo
ignoring the surfers
cresting the waves far below.
The silk flowers could be
our own deaths played out.

Above the laughing blue sea
we can't help looking at them
we need to remind ourselves
that we are not them and
ask again how things might
have been different.

Cartwheeling

The wind howls up the chimney
like the rumbling of bronchitis
how we span out our wheezes
for fun, my brothers and I
as kids will do
and Doctor Miller who knew the
family lungs would prescribe for us
Waterbury's Compound and
postural drainage which
started me on my love of being
upside down to right things
Each year on my birthday
I turn a cartwheel

Adaptation

Another morning,
refuge in the dress
Impossible to wear, to buy
Silk, slippery to the fingers
Transparent crepe with beading
Flesh coloured
Crisp ironed cotton
Splashes of colour
White, creamy, white
What is femininity?
Softness, vulnerability,
The way the fabrics
Slide over the skin
The prohibitive cost
The looks of disdain
From shopgirls.

I'm very dull today
Black on black
With a half-hearted
Touch of purple
I'm not up to anything
More than looking

Head for the haven

Of a coffee lounge

In a bookshop

Grab a few lines

Of poetry along the way

Frost, Keats even

And a new Irish woman

All stretches of silver river

And longing

I'm growing old

The annual reminder

As much as the mirror

And my body's resistance

To camping.

What have I achieved?

I feel stupider than

I was at seventeen

The suitcase I left home with

Sitting miserably in our carport

On the way to

A charity bin,

I don't want its reminder

That once gone

To my surprise

I was forgotten.
After all those years
It was hard to believe
Impossible, almost
But not quite.

I returned a few times
But not many
My spirit lost somewhere
In the city
I'm on my way
To talk about the future
Superannuation
What a funny word
When said slowly.
Christmas will be quiet
For my brother and I
The older ones have
Their spouses' families
And their own
Besides, there's this gap
Two lost in the middle
Cleaving the eight in halves
Now four above, two below.

Nobody pines for the old home
Razed for apartments
The whole town is fast
Disappearing under
Layers of blonde brick
All the old families gone
The Cottiers, the Lakes
The Potts's, the Wegans
The Wakelys, the Herders,
The Louders and Galanders,
Only 'Auntie' left
With her odd shaped block
Where her horse grazed
Near the railway line.

But we made no effort
To save the fibro house
Dad built with mum
Memories are not all good
The days held misery enough
To want to forget.
There's a sad nostalgia
For the small things,
Neighbours nod hello
The biscuit for our dog

An extra chop from the butcher
The annual spectacle
Of a tamed waratah.
Some things were good
But they would change
In any case.
Now it's becoming
A monotony
Of bland yellow boxes
Mum used to sing
That song about
Little boxes on the hillside,
Little boxes all the same.

A place unloved
The ugly duckling
Of the Shire
We knew it for sure
When they ripped up
The row of palms
In Eton Street
And gave them
To Cronulla
For the tourists.
But somehow

It doesn't matter

Things pass

We are glad

We are not

They pass anyway

Families change

People live on

The great gift

Of adaptation

What living is

Without completely forgetting.

Lamb-marking

they're small and soft like toys
and they make quiet little snuffles
perhaps they haven't found their voices yet

we pick them up in a circle pointing out
their woolly bodies resting on our stomachs
and hold their skinny legs apart

then those on the outside
take up their knives with the hooks
and cut off the base of the scrotum
which hardly evokes a sound
but then
we rip out their testicles with the hook
as they squirm like rabbits and if we
can't get them out we get Janine who
grew up on a big station where she learnt
to do it with her teeth

afterwards she looks like she's
just seen the dentist from hell

a quick hole punch in the ear and
all that's left is the tail and
this only takes one quick slice except
when you miss and get a bony bit
and it grates as you cut and it's
more like sawing if the blade's blunt
and they only lose a few usually

before it'll be time for mulesing

Fire Days - January

To: *Duty Officer Bucketty*
7-1 1525
Do you require a channel satellite telephone system. If so contact me asap.

A woman's just back from up north,
she can't get it all out at once,
"M. took over, ignoring the rules,
dragged us to a black area
he noticed as we were dropped in,
if he hadn't, we'd have died."
Fire tornadoes sweep the horizon,
it's all unreal, like a model.
They're asking us head-office people
to go help with radios and logistics.
Someone said the whole second floor's out:
scientists running offices.
The main boss is overlaying the Incident Control System.
Fragments of stories reach us in the city
like blackened leaves,
one gang of fire-fighters pulled out
leaving someone behind.
and the punch line:
maybe they needed more room in the truck.

Lynda's gone.

We watch the sky,

expect the winds to pick up this afternoon.

The building's growing quieter,

bits of radio broadcasts gust past,

weather conditions are expected to deteriorate;

it used to mean rain.

It seems crazy being here in a building full of papers.

There are streams of white smoke down south,

then, a shock, it's much closer;

right near a pile of red-roofed dreams,

a dangerous dark funnel of smoke,

a new outbreak.

Received call approx. 0030 reporting that the fire previously water-bombed by chopper has flared again at portion 2.

Vince says it'll be a lot easier

to get to his fishing spot now.

The Director-General's with the media people next door,

they're fighting for information:

"Is it 26 National Parks now or 27?"

A neighbour walks in to see us:

"I keep getting calls from people saying they want a story to go on in 7 minutes and I say:

`I'm a graphic designer, I can give you a great picture...'"

Vince is gone.

Sunday morning, I get a call.

"Can you be ready in an hour?"

Bankstown cleared us immediately and we were up,

quiet, hardly a run-up,

our pilot watching everywhere,

leaned us right into Peats Ridge,

miles of fire aching to cross the freeway.

At the tiny airport a few pilots hung around,

bitching about air force jockeys and the cricket.

A civil volunteer picked us up, I knew his face,

we'd been at college together in Wagga in 1978.

0245

Spoke to T.H., Sydney electricity, re burning tree at Grid 275328 on D. Road off K. Rd. He said he would arrange for it to be brought down.

We're taken to Erina Fire Control Headquarters,

a nest of crisis organisations,

Victorians, South Australians, wireless experts.

They've been here nearly two weeks,

people are getting tired,

on the weekend they were evacuated.
Hungry crews arrive blacked up and staring in lines,
there's a few women, trying to tread a middle ground
through all the over-stimulated men.
I catch up with one, angry, worn out,
there's a photo of her in the control room
with a caption "Guess what F's saying?"
"I'm walking out halfway through a shift" she says.

We city women, not in uniform,
are stared at, us and the canteen crew
fighting over food for their regiments.
Men lie on floors, slump sideways,
Rambos are still able to strut.
Our contact finds us, we ask how he is.
"I'm here nine days and they give me a day off.
I go surfing and stuff my knee,
can you believe it?"
I ask how they're coping and he lowers his voice,
"There's a whole van down there,
full of psychologists."

1440
Visit from Mayor. Briefed by G. B.

We pile into an office

and are dumped out again.

Yellow overalls and food just keep arriving.

"Come on, who's gonna finish this half of a fresh cream bun?"

One crew wanted something different for breakfast -

"Water and cakes." they said.

"That way we won't be reminded

that another 24 hours has passed."

Two chickadee chick vans stand together for refrigeration,

the generosity's as amazing as the arsonists.

Nobody seems to talk about controlling,

we're chipping carefully at these fires,

going for lives and property.

In a corridor I find Vince, washed-out, dazed,

"The F3's still out," he says,

"We got caught coming up.

It was a mess there yesterday,

some radio station announced it had reopened,

which, for 10 minutes, it did."

1015

Ordered 160 lunches from Central Fire Control for 12 noon. 100 meals for midnight, for delivery on the fire line.

Twenty-two hours straight says Lynda,
I'd just like 8 hours sleep.
They're doing the graveyard shift,
answering calls from people ringing up to say
the fires are out now,
we're just trying to get attention.
We queue behind brigaders at Sizzlers.
Our motel was evacuated yesterday,
the pool's full of ash and leaves.
I ask a motel worker where all the smoke's coming from.
"It's the abbatoir," she said,
"All that fat in the ground, it'll burn for ages."

Night. It actually looks pretty dark,
we turn to see a streak of orange
crackling on the hillside behind.
We watch fuzzy tv news,
fires are moving at Terry Hills, Royal National Park,
the Mountains.
They're saying it may jump the Nepean.
We're told our destination.
"It's hot", they say, "where you're going."

1630

Fire near road at M. catchment. Going to light up from S. Trail to G. N. Road and link dozer trail to further south and light south but no gap between.

We have a bad photocopy of a map to Bucketty.
In our marked car we wave at yellow overalls
on fire trucks and they wave back.
Paddocks are burning themselves out.
When we arrive at the depot, they're not sure what to do,
we haven't done this before and they don't know us.
I got restless and cleaned the bog;
two hundred fire fighters don't think of it.
Finally, we were briefed;
Melanie got radio; I was logistics.

CFA crews come in, black and dirty -
some had their first beer in a week,
played cricket and went home.
"They like a fire, these blokes.
Their boss had ten units - a hundred people -
on the road in one and a half hours from Victoria,
bringing everything with them; control van,
wireless experts, mechanics, cooks.
Use too much water though."
It's the countryside, it's different down there.

They learnt dry firefighting at Bucketty.
We ask after the animals,
they say they are smarter than people think,
sometimes you find baby koalas
in waterholes, afterwards.

2330
Spoke to G. re proposed backburn and he said OK & try to get Slip-ons* back from Upper Hunter.

Melanie and I were the only women.
Crews lie on the floor dozing, days from home,
some just stared and stared.
At times we just had to close the door.
A few tell us about the controlled burning:
CFA were lighting up one side of a rifle range,
National Parks the other,
there were these sounds, ping, ping,
"You should have seen them run."
And the hay shed full of Death Adders,
the farmer hung around, pointing as they slid,
"There goes one, there's another..."

We look at the sky and wait for the next weather report,
Control sends hourly updates,

Relative Humidity, Temperature, Winds
and Fire Danger Index - it's up to 8.
We hear there's more spot fires,
they're plural but we call them "it" anyway:
it's jumped the old convict road where
it's supposed to be stitched in.
They won't use incendiaries now,
they'll go for the next line,
try to hold it at Wollombi Creek.
We learn more:
fires go faster up hill than down,
hot spots happen on road bends,
thick corners of bush, melting cars and people.

1055
G. B. spoke to S. from Central Fire Control and they said 41f Controller said good to see they're all agreeing on something.

The smoke's bad today, really choking,
we sit in the air conditioned office every now and then
for the air.
Crews watch gullies where the fire's
"just creeping down".
People keep turning up:
a journalist comes for his van stranded earlier,

when the F3 was closed,
locals come to see what's going on,
someone brings in a kookaburra he found
on the road at 6 this morning.
We call WIRES and draw straws to see
who gets to wrap him in a towel.
Boxes of eye wash arrive.

More briefings, crew changes picked up
at the airport, more going home.
There's some confusion now,
it's been going so long.
"Where are the dinners?"
"They're arriving here by chopper."
"No, 16 are going to the helipad near S. Creek,"
- a patch of grass in a paddock.
No, a hundred hot dinners turn up and we drive them
to Kulnura Fire control.
We get there and the canteen women say
"We've just fed two hundred of them."
Our boss still hasn't stood down after 9 days
of 18 hours or more. "Soon, soon." he says.
He briefs his relief, but still won't go,
spreads his arms across
the wide red welt on the map.

1730

Temperature 27 Humidity 23 Wind Speed 10.1 Direction 270

We've learnt to take the weather ourselves,
every half hour,
relay it to the men in striker units.
The CFA packed up and left,
they're fighting further down the line,
can't use their big trucks here anymore.
Sitting together in the radio room,
Melanie and I watch for changes in the wind and heat.
Dew point should be reached at 3 am,
this only gives our back-burners till then
to work and then it won't light up anymore.
Another scary day tomorrow high heat and winds -
but it may blow back on itself;
it's out at St Albans.
The Council insists we tell them all the losses in the area.
I fax a vague sheet, 10 houses, three known owners,
not sure of all addresses.

1930

Discussed Q. P. Creek/S. Creek strategy for tonight considering the weather for tomorrow - 37-40C, low RH & NNW winds 15-25 k's.

"This farmer asked me to go and take a look,
he just couldn't.
He had twenty or so cattle in the paddock,
the fire had just blown through.
I went there and there's all these cows just strolling around,
it must have slipped right over the top and missed them."
The visibility's bad again.
A chopper pilot came in and asked us to find out
what channel the other one in the area's using.
We found out though Control,
"Thanks," he said.
"You know, the army's around too, using their own frequencies,
I can't talk to them at all.

Another day, couldn't see 15 feet in front of us,
had to walk before the car so Melanie
could keep it on the road.
Spent the day taking meals out to crews at Stockyard Creek
and the tanker drivers, a few small fires on the way.
We tried to pick up a chainsaw,
"Not with all these widow-makers* around,
we're hanging onto it..."

1010

Owner of "S." where fire truck dropped into seepage pit rang to ask when it will be repaired. Will be in Sydney till Friday. Has left gate open, rope across seepage pit in case another drives into it. Has locked house.

A chopper hit a power line,
saw it just too late and dropped down,
the tail rotor cut and the field exploded into fire.
The pilot was lucky to be alive.
He was also lucky that the Bucketty Bush Fire Brigade
had watched the whole thing
from the steps of the Laguna General Store and Wine Bar,
across the street.

We're starting to blend,
told stories of locals and their families,
the Wisemans', of course, and the many Irish
inbreeding in the valleys,
a school where children hadn't seen a train,
an architect who lectures on permaculture,
the old geezer who kept lazily apologising
about leaving the gate open so his bull
got into their paddocks and their cows,
until they knackered him.
Then there's that family with the goats:

when the son left the valley,
the robberies stopped.

0220
CFA advises that they are patrolling G. D. Drive from M. Creek Road to S. Track - some tall trees still burning - checking for sparks.

Things are winding down here.
We take more meals out ourselves.
Drive the skinny dozer trail for two hours
stopping at each truck with it's crew of two,
finally, we reach a small valley,
four men stand near their striker units
looking up at the hillsides, black and empty,
they describe how fires "crown" from ridge to ridge.

Someone says, "You have to laugh sometimes.
One bloke thought someone had moved his boat,
it was his trailer all right,
with a puddle of aluminium under it."

The next morning, the boss who wouldn't go home
had trouble getting the mattress off his back.
The new man has been a fire boss before,
he writes more.
The night crew had left early.
We're locked out at 7 am with the Council delivery man
and 10 drums of Avgas for the choppers.
On our car's radio Control can hear us,
but we can't hear them.
I listen to a truck's radio inside the compound,
luckily, it's turned up loud,
I relay messages to Melanie who repeats it
into the mouthpiece, saying
"Copy, Bucketty Depot, Cessnock Control."

0215
Perimeter burning complete on two properties. Reconnaissance carried out on additional three properties at S.C.

We have to wait for someone with a key.
"You can't leave anything lying around here anymore,"
says the driver,
"Avgas outside the gate for instance.
"I live in Pokolbin," he says,

"Never used to lock anything up.
My old Aunt had to go into a nursing home.
People came and broke all the windows in her house,
ripped the doors off from the inside,
took the mantlepiece,
chopped the top off an old tank;
it's probably blacked-up and hanging in a restaurant somewhere."
He names the birds differently to the books:
Leather Heads, Asian Starling, Mountain Lowrie.

1500
Bulga attempting to back burn O. C. Road to W. Creek.

Help arrives and we're in.
Things are cooling down,
we'll be going home soon.
For them there's a new fire to worry about,
it's somewhere to the west,
when they first heard about it
it was far away and unthinkable,
on the map they drew a vague shape
and called it "Boo".
It's closing in.
A plane flew over some burning houses
just as drums of fuel exploded

shooting flames way up into the air.
Nearly scared the pilot to death.

1130

Army chopper arrives - Sea King - "these are useless"

Fire Day 12.1

We stop at someone's home on the way,
drink tea from china cups.
On SBS News a *man runs from his house*
with a television set.
"In Bosnia the leaders are starving their own people to death. They won't let the food convoys through. They are selling what they can't eat for food, those with nothing to sell, don't eat."

The Harbour looks like nothing's happened;
sailing boats skim,
white against all that blue water.
I'm thirsty.
We meet our friends and relatives
but have nothing to say.

At home, I guess the temperature, humidity, wind speed.
I'm pretty close.

* Notes:

Slip-ons = small water tanker units

Widow-maker = tree burnt-out inside and in danger of falling

Striker Unit = 4wd truck with slip-on

Two Red Chickens

Two red chickens live out their lives
in a barn, for their eggs.
They lay few now, bred for a brief
but profitable life.
In commerce they'd be retired,
like superseded washing machines,
or a mistress grown wrinkled.

Two warm bundles of surprises.
If only they didn't peck or shit
they'd be perfect.

The valley of soundless trees: Wollombi

We hike through the Eggs and Bacon
scratch our legs on native holly
the track dissolves and reforms
towards the end of a spur
a meeting-ledge for ghosts.

We bring our morning faces and
unfolding bodies to the valley
of soundless trees, spreading
their limbs in the emptiness
fruiting for themselves alone.

Through delicate shadows the fluid body
of the bay vibrates, sea of broken glass.
Grevillia tentacles reach out to me from
a different focus, bottle brush, fiery red;
my thermos steams with apple-scented tea.

From nowhere springs a wind to clear my head,
sweeps clear the crystals turning the sea
to living ultramarine, support for all the fishes,
all the boats carrying cargo for dreamers.

A sudden silence: an absence of the low hum
as traffic stops at the bridge opening.
A yachtful of people pass through.
Our efforts cease, people get out of cars.
For a few minutes, old technology
interrupts and we have time to wonder.

At the gallery we wondered and wondered
at reluctant Aboriginal women with painted
breasts, unable to reach us with their dance.
Two unsteady performances, then they stopped.
A few pulled on bras. They unrolled a painting
to try to help us see.

Afterwards, they didn't go away.
They stayed, wanted to talk, shake hands,
laugh with us, people, no longer an audience.
But we didn't stay, went back
to our offices, wondering.

The White Plumed Honeyeater

A shard of grey and lime green flashes past
the bird is back, building a nest
in the bottlebrush, only to have it
torn apart by marauding bullies:
wattlebirds.
But it will try again, beneath the roar of jet engines,
beside the shopping mall, close to railway lines
and roads choking with city fumes.
The little bundle flies off to find a better place:
giving in doesn't occur to birds.

bee   yellow   native

how many more faces are there in the city
so many
like Sack's woman who remembered everything
as she walked down the street
I should jump into alleys to let it assimilate
but I'm exhausted just seeing us all

lunch time
the park is luscious with neglected grass
growing long and wild   accompliced by renegade mallow
heartweed and dandelions
I'm frightened at how distant I've become from it all
in my flat with my potted memories around me
a bee lands near my foot   yellow   native
there's a serenity here despite the dull moan
of traffic behind the trees
an insect could live out its whole life oblivious to it
if only
I roll back the cuff of my jacket
grab my bag

Winter

all those smooth hills

that peace and

quiet

with cows

overlapping and intertwining

and religious

spirits move

together

at the clouding

of the moon

evening vomits frost

all around

as lovers kill

each other

beneath red stars

folding their hands

about

the scented air

bringing it to their

mouths

they kiss

Garden

mauve-fleshed wisteria
pour their
liquid light
onto lovers
darkened
by their
green leaf shadows
hiding
from the sky

splashes of
dew and saliva
every centimetre
on alert
they hold each
other's face
for something
tangible

There are no bells, it's just the sound of restaurant lanterns in Chinatown

(Summer visit to the Chinese Garden, Darling Harbour, Sydney)

Near the

fragrance

pavilion pink

lotus petals

spread through

thick, unstirring

heat, almost

touching distant

white blossoms,

overblown.

leaves saucer

below, even

these three

feet in

the air. a

camera clicks.

I tread
the laid path.
blue-bodied
dragonflies shoot
here and there,
a duck ripples
through, nudging
small bundles
of water to
cliffs in a
miniature landscape.
if I never
lifted my eyes,
could I have
a life
without winter?

A carnival toy,
the monorail
corrupts the peace
of willows.
I seek shelter
in a bamboo
forest pavilion.
through its
cracked-ice panes
a bulbul,
eye to eye,
sings but
is silenced
by a distortion
of electric guitars

All flowers

blend. one

peach hibiscus

ruffles the mauve

crepe myrtle,

their substance,

not colours,

in harmony.

it's getting

too warm now.

escaping the

path I touch

one Sage in

the Forest who

is not cold.

Gardenia and
frangipani entwine
their offerings
in the air.
the coolness
of the aquatic
pavilion is
overwhelming.
I sit.
everywhere tiny
fish pierce the
surface. across
the light-filled
water, below
the tough shells
of commerce,
rests a stone

Mountain track alone

Marker G4 says, No Way Through Go Back.
A ship-sized rock has splayed the path,
I stop warily at the sight,
for some minutes of peace.

A whip bird nearby is answered elastically
by his mate. Cloud-screened light falls down
to the valley where bellbird chimes float
Christmas to the tomb-grey cliffs above.

Cockatoos in the distance drop like confetti:
I want to explore the pathless wilds,
as if freedom only exists in these valleys
with their deceptive cheerfulness, safe

from the wind chiselling the escarpment.
I look up at its stern red face,
pale cloud fragments across the sky,
no-one else has passed this way.

Myall Lakes

I: At the camp

We almost bump into a kookaburra,
he leapt up, around, turned his anvil-beak away,
and eyed us straight.
Mother sugar-glider backpacks
her long-eared child down for bread;
black ducks swim aimlessly by.
Boys with panel vans set up camp,
light a fire against warning,
tossing on branches for fun.
Sparks shoot high into the night air
but we don't get involved:
city-dwellers are lost in the wilderness.
A goanna, blamed for stealing our chicken-ends
moves in for more in broad daylight,
its speckled body sleek to ground.
It waits, watches,
weighs hunger against risk.

II: Canoeing

Three spoonbills eye us stiffly,
over the reeds;
we sail into the green spikes.

A host of black swans rise at our approach,
wingbeats drumming the surface.
We cross the bay against the breeze,
cursing the splash at the bow,
the shore not coming closer.
Then, finally, land:
sweep of white sand and blackened forest.
Roasted banksia pods have released
their issue in middens of burnt bottles.
Trunks of charred trees exude
red flushes of life.
But there's a sense of loss
and smoky death.

III: At the summit
From the halfway view, the islands form
a horizon of welcoming curves,
soft shoulders for a mariner lost in a fog.
Cool air plays along the cliff - could we
live here forever without help?
We climb higher.
There's a lake up north, way up,
long slice of silver,
the cliffs conceal
old pockets for artillery,

Now, there's just one island
through the elegant shrubs;
bottlebrush and broom.
Way below, the uneven surf
crashes against hackly brown cliffs,
swirls of black weed and rocks
disturb the clear jade,
white, white horses stroll
towards them across the depths:
a butterfly passes through.

River Swim

Push through warm
golden glass water
pull pull
arms curve out
stir ripples
a cormorant lands
watches, dives
gains a fish
from my world

lifts to the air

pull pull

breathe breathe

carmine dragonfly

before my hippo-eyes

I'm a water snake

I'm a turtle

the midday bush

sings with insects

thut, thut

paddles ease past

smooth-muscled Peppermints

yellow-green leaves

fall to a mirror -

the sky.

Return of the Shearwaters

The sun is swallowed by the bloody sea,
night drops darkness and briny air,
children fidget, make anxious noises,
the rest of us silent in the foreign land
of night. Then it begins:
graceful arcs over waves
full bellies for the nest,
near invisible thud after thud
in blackness eyes strain to track
the comforting bulk for a hungry settler:
Muttonbirds.
Their thuds dissipate the hiss of waves,
chill of cooling sand, the undefined space
of the dark beach.
This is their struggle web-footed,
built for flying: we listen for the final silence
safe in their nests, then drift away
hands reaching for one another.

Spring at Bronte

the sea
seaside seaside sounds
rolling down meadows
to water's edge
cries up above
big-headed gulls
red eyes glisten in
sun fished from the
sea
seaside seaside sea
strolling through
cracked face headlands
wizened sandstone
en route to sand
in the sea
seaside seaside
styrene cups collide
in rocky cloisters
guard subdued waves
fragrant spray swirls
up to rubber thick leaves
seaside seaside
yellow

flowers spread like honey

bodies like jellyfish

Unchanging territory - The Snowy, for Mike

I

Through snow gums twisting their rainbow trunks

the three of us take off for a slight incline

we call a slope.

Slip, slide, fall, slush.

A few seconds on two even skis;

almost gliding.

Higher, higher, we clump our fish-scaled slats

into crunchy white ice, a fraction less balance

and they slip from beneath us:

fall, laugh.

The pure pleasure of beginning: never again

can we be so recklessly bad at it.

We risk higher and higher levels on our beginners'

run over skidoo tracks. Tramp, tramp,

Mike walks for a while,

a break from the effort of learning.

But soon he suggests a real journey

`to that patch of licheny rocks, over there'.

John takes the lead; up, up, crunch, crunch -

even climbing a pleasure. We cut, embarrassed,

across waiting downhillers,

but kids on toboggans lift our egos.

Let's zig-zag, I call,

(later from a book we learn the right words)

II

Back to base; fall, crash, laugh,

a drink at our lodge,

the luxury of a warm wooden deck over snow,

photos. We cook our meal,

spreading out through the open-plan,

watching rabbits through big wasteful windows:

smelling garlic, onion, butter.

Others arrive, downhillers.

A mother sweeps in and turns on

the fan over our stove.

It's her stove.

at her end of the kitchen.
The men grab beers and the fire.

The silence breaks; we swap naivety
for experience as she unpacks their food.
Our meal is ready. Mike likes the chicken,
breading out the sauce.
We move our mess. She reclaims the stove,
instructing two teenagers in a brittle voice.

III
Suddenly, it's dark.
Mike fossicks a library of star-clad magazines.
John talks to our neighbours (they're neighbours),
in the warm lamplight I'm writing this poem.
The women clean up with the kids,
and show us the dishwasher.

Last Days at Work

I

Venetian-sliced action invites me
to the horizon far away,
behind the voluptuous headlands.
Columns of light spear thunder-clouds
through to the water below.
From my skyscraper crow's nest
I survey the growing squall;
the gathering of white restless horses.

I want to put it all together,
disappear down some telescopic sight,
see further, be further away
from the circular track of commerce,
the order of government.
Take me to the boundlessness of the sea,
the eternal temptation to sailors
with its lifelong guarantee of the unexpected.

II

The sea is dull as yesterday;
it lies in leaden slumber around the choking shores

where human machinations poke here and there through
the polluted haze of a humid Sydney lunchtime.
Boats crawl like silver-track slugs;
one, another, until, almost imperceptibly, a sailing boat,
christened `tall ship' by Bicentennial sellers,

displays its antique gait through the grey viscosity,
then disappears, discreetly, behind steel and plastic.

III
(Bogongs)

They migrate now to office towers
as if the city was a dark mountain wilderness
and to some it is.
Within it there's a remoteness
from humanity and an emptiness
as vast as any gorge, and a feeling
that although you think you know
where you are and why you are here
perhaps you never did after all.

IV

I'm so high the gardens are toys
with plastic rose beds and perfect palms.
It's all in perspective, contained within
this window's black metal frame.

Like a postcard, everything fits, from the fountain
where kookaburras squat on Governor Philip
to the restless sea beyond the heads,
still something like their shape in old drawings,
following 18th century waterlines.

If only they had high towers then they could
see the wind's subtle work so much clearer -
the surface spreads with cowlicks and Irish promises,
sheets of light rippling from side to side,
like Japan fans, or secret eyes, or Christmas.

V

Today the sea rustles into

it's starlet's sequinned dress,
urging it sensually over
the undulating energy below.

Here and there the land buts in
nudges of vegetation,
but it's lost in the glistening
of a thousand press shots.

Beneath, the depths are blue,
reflections of the most innocent eyes,
even if they are only lenses.

VI

Sunlight sprawls lazily over its old friend, the harbour.
It picks at crests of water and bakes the terracotta roofs
on a far off peninsular.
After rain, we can see to the horizon,
but it will fade if the heat continues,
haze will rise across the surface to mix with
all the outpourings of chimneys and cars and lungs
trapped in this earth-basin,
until another restless wind ushers in showers from nowhere.

VII

Green salad gardens
swirl with plant oils
and orange-peel perfume
from picnickers
in office-dress

You almost wish a
blue Cronulla wave
high as the 7th Floor
would wash over it,
leaving it refreshed.

Instead, it steams hazily
on through the day,
until a thick cloud hangs
across the falling sun,
drowning in the west.

VIII

(Crane)

Each straining metal rise
pierces the fairylight rain
slanting through the afternoon.
It engulfs the emptiness,
the gasp of office mouths.

In one breath I'm on a bus,
the crane comes down,
finally, to rest.

Made in the USA
Columbia, SC
10 December 2022